JANE'S

HISTORICAL AIRCRAFT

1902-1916

DOUBLEDAY & COMPANY, INC.
GARDEN CITY, NEW YORK

Copyright © Jane's Yearbooks: Macdonald & Co (Publishers) Ltd 1972

Originally published in 1917 by Sampson Low, Marston & Co Ltd
First published in this edition in 1972 by Jane's, Macdonald & Co
(Publishers) Ltd, Paulton House, Shepherdess Walk, London N.1.

Doubleday edition, 1973
Library of Congress Catalog Card Number 72-88700
ISBN : 0-385 01314-0

Printed in Great Britain by
Redwood Press Limited
Trowbridge, Wiltshire

PUBLISHER'S NOTE

Fred Jane was a man of great perspicacity. In 1909 he published JANE'S ALL THE WORLD'S AIRSHIPS (AEROPLANES AND DIRIGIBLES), cataloguing the products of the then infant aircraft industry. By 1917 the book, now retitled JANE'S ALL THE WORLD'S AIRCRAFT, was firmly established as an annual work of reference, developments in the aviation field having exceeded anything that might have been foreseen in the year of its inception—except, that is, by a few pioneers such as Fred Jane. In this year of 1917, at the height of the First World War which had led to further aeronautical progress, it was felt that the history of aviation was now long enough, and important enough, to warrant a special section in the annual reference book.

This section, with its uniquely valuable record of the early days of aviation, is here reproduced intact, in the belief that it forms an historical document of outstanding interest. An aeronautical dictionary from the same volume is also reproduced, for the same reason.

In order to preserve the flavour of the original, no corrections of any kind have been made to the text.

ALL THE WORLD'S HISTORICAL AIRCRAFT,

FROM 1902 TO 1916.

WITH HISTORICAL PREFACES ON "WAR BALLOONS AND PARACHUTES,"

BY THE

COUNTESS OF DROGHEDA,

AND "A BRIEF HISTORY OF MODERN AERONAUTICS," BY

C. G. GREY.

HISTORICAL PREFACES.

WAR BALLOONS—1794-1865.

(By the Countess of Drogheda).

[The following articles are taken, by kind permission of the talented authoress, from the descriptive catalogue of the Exhibition of Historical Pictures collected and arranged by the Countess of Drogheda in 1917. Lady Drogheda has made a special study of War Balloons and Parachutes, and the information hereafter may be taken as historically accurate.—Editor.]

In view of the paramount importance of the "Command of the Air" in modern warfare it is only natural to ask what were the earlier attempts to put the aircraft of the day to military use. Fortunately a detailed account of the first experiments of this nature is to be found in that invaluable book, "Astra Castra," and these few lines aim at giving the briefest possible summary of a chapter from that work for the benefit of any who may be interested in the subject. No one will be surprised to learn that it was in the French army that the first Flying Corps was formed, but probably few people realize that it was as early as 1794, only a year after the execution of Louis XVI, that a war-balloon was actually employed in battle.

The honour of suggesting the experiment appears to belong to the savants of the French Academy, under whose auspices an Aeronautic School was established at Meudon, directed by Captain (afterwards Colonel) Coutelle, of the Republican Army, who soon constructed four hot-air balloons, specially appropriated to the different divisions of the French Army—viz., the "Entreprenant" for the army of the North; the "Céleste" for that of the Sambre and Meuse; the "Hercule" for the army of the Rhine and Moselle; and the "Intrépide" for the army of Egypt.

Colonel Coutelle himself was sent by the Committee of Public Safety to Maubeuge, where he was received with great suspicion and nearly shot as a spy by Duquesnez, the Commissioner of the Convention with the Army of the North, whose duty it was to "see that soldiers went into battle, and to force the generals to conquer under menace of the guillotine." He managed, however, to allay Duquesnez's suspicions, and on June 26, 1794, actually ascended in the "Entreprenant" at the battle of Fleurus, where his observations were of great assistance to General Jourdan, though the balloon was probably of even greater service through its effect on the morale of the Austrians, who are said to have been greatly discouraged by the knowledge that all their movements could be seen, while they were in ignorance of what the French were doing.

Colonel Coutelle's achievement at this battle appears to have excited great admiration amongst the Austrians, for when later on he was sent to Mannheim with a flag of truce, an Austrian officer received him with the words: "Monsieur l'Ingénieur Aërien, les Autrichiens savent honorer les talents et la bravoure; vous serez traité avec distinction, c'est moi qui vous ai aperçu et signalé le premier, pendant la bataille de Fleurus, au Prince Coburg, dont je suis l'aide-de-camp."

It is from a report by the same Colonel Coutelle that we learn that "the Aerostat, commanded by Captain Hammond (No. 1 Company of the Aerostatic Corps), which many shells and balls could not compel to descend at Ehrenbreitstein, was riddled by bullets near Frankfort."

Two of Coutelle's balloons could still be seen in 1856, one in Vienna, and the other at Metz. The Aerostatic Corps came, however, to a premature end, for Napoleon, after using war balloons in Egypt, allowed the Meudon establishment to languish without support until 1802 or 1804, when he finally abolished it.

After the French had ceased to persevere with this new branch of the army, no further experiments in military aviation appear to have been made until Napoleon's Russian campaign, and then, strangely enough, not by the French but by the Russians. On entering Moscow, in 1812, the French soldiers found in the Castle of Voronzoff a large aerostat containing many thousands of pounds of gunpowder which were to have been launched upon them. General Count Philip de Ségur says: "This prodigious balloon was constructed by command of Alexander, not far from Moscow, under the direction of a German artificer. The destination of this winged machine was to hover over the French army, to single out its chief, and to destroy him by a shower of balls and fire. Several attempts were made to raise it, but without success, the springs by which the wings were to be worked having always broken."

Efforts were made to revive the use of aerostats in the French African campaign of 1830, but there seems to have been no opportunity to employ them in that war.

The Austrians are said to have been the next to employ observation balloons—before Venice in 1849—and the Russians used them in observing from Sebastopol. Various suggestions for their adaptation by the British Army appear to have been made during the Crimean War, but as an officer writing in 1862 puts it: "Though the *principle* of these schemes was highly approved of by the officers to whom they were referred, and though similar propositions have been repeatedly made since that time, it is hardly necessary to mention that balloons have hitherto never been used for military purposes in the British service. Their absence from our field equipment is probably more attributable to an over-estimate of their defects, than to a non-appreciation of their advantages in military operations."

The French again employed balloons during the Italian campaign of 1859—this time under the direction of two civilian aeronauts, the brothers Godard—who made ascents from Milan, the Castiglione hills and other points, but the results are said to have proved great failures from the military point of view. It is interesting though to note that there was a considerable controversy at this time as to the respective merits of Montgolfières (hot-air balloons) or Charlières (gas balloons), the balance of opinion being very naturally in favour of the Charlières, though both were so imperfect that Lieutenant Grover, R.E., in the report which he drew up in 1862 was abundantly justified in saying: "The more, then, that we examine the investigations into the subject that have been conducted by foreign officers . . . the more do we become convinced that there has not been yet discovered a satisfactory system of military ballooning, one fit (that is to say) to satisfy all the evident exigencies of actual warfare."

In the American Civil War balloons were used by the Federal Army, a balloon staff commanded by Professor Low being attached to General McClellan's army, but one gathers the impression that the results attained were not of much value. The following *resumé* of the balloon-corps and apparatus with General McClellan's army is, however, interesting for purposes of comparison :—

BALLOON CORPS.

1 Chief Aeronaut	Requiring
1 Captain, assistant aeronaut	2 instructed
50 Non-commissioned officers and privates	men.

APPARATUS.

2 Generators, drawn by 4 horses each
2 Balloons, ,, ,, 4 horses each (including tools, spare ropes, etc.)
1 Acid-cart, ,, ,, 2 horses.

Gambetta's escape from Paris in a balloon during the siege of 1871, and the employment of aircraft in more modern times, are too well-known to require mention here.

THE EARLIEST PARACHUTE DESCENTS, 1783-1837.

(By The Countess of Drogheda.)

The modern parachute has proved itself to be so efficient as a means of saving life during the present war that many who are interested in aviation may be glad to read a few brief details of the earlier parachute descents. It cannot, of course, be said that the parachute has developed much in the last few years. The apparatus is indeed too simple for it to be capable of much development, and modern parachutes are so efficient that even minor mishaps during descents are nowadays almost unknown, and it is only by the greatest misfortune that a fatal accident can occur. One such accident is fresh in all our minds, when Captain Basil Hallam, through some cause which has not hitherto been made public, lost his life when leaping from a kite balloon which had broken from its moorings and was being driven by the wind towards the German lines.

Descent after descent is however now made with perfect safety, and the parachute can with absolute truth be described to-day, as it was—with less truth—described many years ago, as the life-belt of the air; and when, in the near future, we travel from place to place in great passenger airships, the aerial companies will doubtless be compelled to carry a sufficient number of parachutes in case of accidents.

So much for the modern parachutes, but what of the parachutes of a hundred years ago? The principle on which it was constructed was, it is true, the same as that of to-day; but safety can hardly be said to have been the chief characteristic of the earlier parachutes, and he was indeed a bold man who first let himself fall from the (exceedingly dangerous) hot-air balloon in which he had ascended. The accounts which have been preserved of the first experiments in parachutes are neither very numerous nor very detailed, and it is possible that some descents may have been made of which no records have been kept; but enough remains to fill us with profound admiration for the brave men who, with the imperfect material at their disposal, risked or lost their lives in the experiments which alone have made possible the parachute of to-day.

The first account of something resembling a parachute descent occurs in M. de la Loubère's history of Siam, which he visited in 1687. In it he speaks of "an ingenious athlete who exceedingly diverted the King and his Court by leaping from a height and supporting himself in the air by two umbrellas, the handles of which were affixed to his girdle."

The honour of making the first real parachute descent belongs, however, to a Frenchman, M. le Normand, who in 1783 jumped from the height of a first story holding in his hand a parachute, 30 inches in diameter, which broke the force of the fall so much that he was hardly sensible of any shock upon reaching the ground. From this experiment, we are told, M. le Normand calculated that a parachute 14 feet in diameter would afford complete protection to a man descending from the height of the clouds.

It was reserved for the celebrated aeronaut, Jean Pierre Blanchard, to make the first parachute descent which attracted general attention, and Blanchard was also the inventor to whom the construction of parachutes attached to balloons may be attributed. In his first experiment Blanchard let fall a dog from the height of 6,000 feet in the course of an ascent which he made from Strasbourg, and the animal reached the ground without the least injury. In 1793 Blanchard made a parachute descent himself at Basle, but owing to some mishap the apparatus failed to act properly and his fall was so rapid that he broke his leg. It is interesting to note that Blanchard announced that his object in adapting parachutes for use with balloons was to enable the aeronaut to escape in case of accident by fire or otherwise.

It was not until October 21st, 1797, that the first completely successful descent from a considerable height was made, the hero of the exploit being the famous French aeronaut, André Jacques Garnerin, who eventually lost his life when attempting a similar descent in France. M. Garnerin was also the first aeronaut to descend from a parachute in England. The date was September 21st, 1802, and the contemporary records of the experiment state that the descent was made "from an amazing elevation." The parachute appears to have fallen for some seconds with ever-increasing speed, and to have oscillated so widely that the basket or cage containing Garnerin seemed at times to be almost horizontal. Garnerin passed over Mary-le-Bone and Somers Town, and almost grazed the houses of St.

Pancras. He actually landed in a field near the Jew's Harp Tavern, but so severe was the shock that it threw him violently to the ground and cut his face. He also bled considerably from the ears and nose. He appeared to be much agitated, and "trembled exceedingly" when released from the basket. One of the stays of the parachute had indeed given way, thus deranging the apparatus and disturbing its proper balance, so that Garnerin was fortunate to reach the earth in comparative safety.

The following details of his parachute have been preserved:— It was made of some cotton material and shaped like an umbrella; a round hoop eight feet in diameter ran round the top, and the sides when expanded were about fifteen feet long and formed a kind of curtain.

Perhaps the most interesting of the earlier descents was that made on July 24th, 1808, by R. Jordarki Kuparanto, who ascended from Warsaw in a Montgolfière (or fire balloon) and narrowly escaped destruction through his balloon catching fire. He was, however, able to descend on his parachute, and this is certainly the first, and probably the only time till the twentieth century that a parachute actually proved to be a life-belt in the air.

In September, 1815, Eliza Garnerin, a great lady-aeronaut, ascended from Paris and descended in a parachute.

It was many years after this that fresh experimentalists, introducing parachutes constructed on new and faulty lines, met with death or disaster.

The most famous of these descents of which any record has been kept was the fatal one made in July, 1837, by Mr. Robert Cocking. This descent acquired great notoriety, and was described in considerable detail by contemporary writers, besides forming the subject of numerous pictures. It is of special interest, because the parachute which Mr. Cocking invented was constructed on an entirely novel principle. It resembled an umbrella turned inside out, the inventor's idea apparently being that this would prevent the oscillations during the descent which were the main drawback to the parachutes invented by Garnerin and others.

The ascent was made from the Vauxhall Gardens, the parachute being attached to the Great Nassau Balloon, and the balloon was over Blackheath when spectators saw Mr. Cocking detach the parachute, which started to descend with great rapidity, accompanied by fearful oscillations. Mr. Cocking's body fell near here. He was still alive, but died in a few seconds. Two accounts of the descent have come down to us. The first is by a man who observed it through a telescope from Sydenham Common, who gives the following details:—

"At twenty-three minutes to eight the balloon and parachute ascended steadily from the Gardens, appearing to pass along without the least oscillation. Mr. Cocking appeared distant from the car of the balloon about three-fourths the height of the balloon. The parachute in form was that of an inverted cone, with its sides from the apex to the base slightly convex; at seven minutes to eight, when it was detached from the

balloon, its sides, from the apex to the base then appeared slightly concave, descending very steadily for about ten seconds, when it appeared to enter a cloud and was lost to sight for about ten seconds; it then emerged from beneath the cloud, and continued to descend as steadily as when first separated from the balloon for about forty seconds, its distance then being, I should judge, from the earth, about one mile, when the upper rim of the parachute suddenly collapsed and its descent instantly became more rapid, and it descended with such accelerated velocity that I did not keep it in sight more than five seconds. The whole time that elapsed in its descent from its separation from the balloon to the time I lost sight of it, was one minute and ten seconds, and at the time it was detached from the balloon I should judge it was full one mile and a quarter from the earth."

The second account is by Mr. Charles Green, one of the family of three who went up in the Nassau Balloon on this occasion. He states that he caused a trial to be made, with a view to ascertain whether the buoyancy of the balloon was sufficient to carry up the parachute with safety, and that the result was satisfactory after 650 pounds of ballast had been given up. He had, however, on several occasions expressed his determination not to liberate the parachute from the balloon, upon the ground that he might select a moment for the severance when Mr. Cocking was not altogether prepared or ready for the descent, so it was arranged that they should ascend to an elevation of a mile and a quarter, and that Mr. Cocking should then detach himself; but it was only with difficulty that the balloon reached that height after discharging 50 pounds more ballast. When all was ready, Mr. Cocking was asked if he felt himself quite comfortable, and whether he found that the practical trial bore out the calculations he had made. He replied, "Yes! I never felt more comfortable or more delighted in my life." Shortly afterwards, Mr. Cocking said, "Well, now, I think I shall leave you," to which Mr. Green replied: "I wish you a good-night and safe descent if you are determined to make it, and not use the tackle."* Scarcely were these words uttered before a slight jerk upon the liberating iron was felt, but Mr. Cocking had failed in the attempt to free himself; another, but more powerful, jerk followed, and in an instant the balloon "shot upwards with the velocity of a sky-rocket."

A coroner's inquest was held on the body, and the following verdict was given:—"We find the deceased, Robert Cocking, came to his death casually, and by misfortune, in consequence of serious injuries which he received from a fall in a parachute of his own invention and contrivance which was appended to a balloon, and we further find that the parachute, as moving towards his death, is deodand and forfeit to our Sovereign Lady the Queen."

*An apparatus has been constructed with a view to prevent any accident arising, in the event of the violence of the wind rendering it impossible for a descent to be attempted, so that Mr. Cocking could haul himself up into the car of the balloon; and this is the tackle alluded to.

A BRIEF HISTORY OF MODERN AERONAUTICS.

(By C. G. Grey.)

Writing a history of aeronautics within the scope of an introduction to a section of this work is rather like writing the Lord's Prayer on the back of a threepenny bit. Still, one can but do one's best, and if the result is rather sketchy the blame must fall on " exigencies of space."

Setting aside the French gentlemen of the early 19th Century who endeavoured to paddle their own balloon by hand, the first really successful aerial navigator of a power-driven balloon was Senor Santos Dumont, a Brazilian sportsman, who built and navigated his miniature airships in Paris. Several Frenchmen, notably the Robert Frères and MM. Giffard, Dupuy de Lôme, Tissandier and Rénard, and a couple of Germans, had had minor successes, but had all come to a violent end, or had escaped injury by dying in their beds previously.

Following on the successes of Santos, various balloonists took to airship making, notably the Lebaudy Frères, who were sugar millionaires by profession and balloonists for sport. They built and are still building many more or less successful ships, up to 1,000 horse-power apiece. M. Clément, the famous motor maker, also took to airships, and by combining his engines with envelopes made by the Astra Company and the Zodiac Company—both formerly makers of balloons—he has produced between 1909 and to-day a number of fine ships.

In England the late Mr. S. F. Cody produced, in conjunction with Colonel (now General) Capper, R.E., a quaint sausage-shaped affair called the " Nulli Secundus," which blew away in a gale after voyaging from Aldershot over London to the Crystal Palace in 1907. The mishap produced a suggestion in " Punch " that the next effort should be called the " Nulli Tertius," so anyhow the British tax-payer received a good joke for his money.

The first real British success was a tiny airship built by Mr. E. T. Willows, practically single-handed, at Cardiff. His first experimental ship was made in 1904-5, and included a clever arrangement for swivelling his propellers so that they could pull the ship up or down. The idea was adopted in subsequent officially built airships. Late in 1909 Mr. Willows piloted his airship from Cardiff to London, and in November, 1910, in the same ship with a new envelope, Mr. Willows, accompanied by his mechanic Goodden, flew across to France, eventually reaching Paris, and was the first airship pilot to cross the Channel.

Beginning again in 1909 the Royal Aircraft Factory at Farnborough made some small airship experiments. These developed, and by 1912-13, with the help of a few keen aeronauts like Captain Maitland, Essex Regiment; and Lieutenants Waterlow and Fletcher, R.E., the little Army airships did valuable work, and were eventually taken over by the Navy.

Up to 1914 the Navy's only attempt was the ill-fated " Mayfly," which broke at Barrow. During the War a number of small patrol airships have been produced, but till this date (November, 1916), the two best " British " ships have been an Astra Torres, and one Parseval airship, purchased in France and Germany respectively, about a year before the outbreak of war.

Italy has produced some very good little airships, which have done well in the war. None of the smaller countries have done anything. Even America and Russia have paid no serious attention to airships.

Germany is the spiritual and substantial home of the real airships. In and after 1907 Major von Gross produced many useful airships, which were built by the Army and known as the " M " (or Militärische) type. Major von Parseval began experiments in 1906, and by 1912 was building ships able to carry twenty people at 50 miles an hour. Parseval airships were sold to Russia, Italy, and England, as well as to the German Army and Navy.

Germany's triumph is, of course, the Zeppelin, designed by Count von Zeppelin, who began experimenting in 1900. Despite misfortunes of fire, wind, and finance he struggled gamely on, and by 1913 had produced eighteen ships, each an improvement on its predecessor. The passenger ships of 1913 carried a matter of twenty-four passengers and a crew of a dozen or so, and the warships of to-day carry a crew of twenty-two or twenty-three, and probably a couple of tons of bombs, besides fuel for between twelve and twenty-four hours' running. Their speed is about 70 miles an hour, and, despite adverse criticism, their military and naval value is high. The latest Zeppelin embodies many external characteristics of the Schütte-Lanz, a ship developed later than the early Zeppelin, and built of wood instead of aluminium, though not because of any shortage of aluminium in Germany. The Zeppelins brought down in Essex last year by the R.F.C. are the latest, if not the last, word in airship design.

Aviation History.

Giving full credit to Daedalus, Icarus, Leonardo da Vinci, Sir George Cayley and his coachman, and the early gliding experiments of Lilienthal, Chanute, Pilcher and others, we arrive at the fact that the first person to fly on a machine heavier than air and driven by its own power was Orville Wright, who after numerous gliding experiments without an engine, and after sundry abortive attempts with an engine, actually took the air in a controlled flight on December 17th, 1903, at Dayton, Ohio, U.S.A. He piloted the machine after drawing lots with his brother Wilbur for the pleasure and honour of this first flight.

The Wrights came to Europe late in 1908, and showed Europeans how to fly, though prior to their arrival some tentative hops had been made, first by Ellehammer, a Dane, then by Santos-Dumont, of airship fame, then by Henry Farman, and

a shade later by Louis Bleriot ; but none of these had flown as the Wrights flew. A. V. Roe and S. F. Cody also left the ground in England in 1908.

However, the quick French mind soon saw where the Wrights scored in their design, and by the middle of 1909 the Wright was already a back number. And, curiously enough, despite American ingenuity and engineering resources, American aeroplanes have never regained that brief lead they held for a few months in 1908. France and England, conjointly or alternately, have led the world ever since in aeroplane design, and Germany has always been a trifle in front in aero-engines, thanks to the encouragement given by the Emperor and the German Government to German engine designers.

It has in fact become a standing joke that England is always six months ahead of Germany in design and twelve months behind in deliveries.

From the early efforts of Farman and Bleriot sprang the two distinctively French types of aeroplane, the " pusher " biplane, with pilot and passenger in front, and engine and propeller behind, which developed from the Farman " box-kite," and the " tractor " monoplane with engine and airscrew in front, which descends directly from the Bleriot.

The introduction by the Brothers Séguin of the Gnome rotary engine at the Great Reims Meeting in August, 1909, completely revolutionised flying, for, whereas, before an aeroplane had to be fairly efficient to be lifted by the heavy engines then existing, the Gnome was so light itself that it was able to drag any clumsy old thing off the ground, so experimenters were enabled to go up into the air and experiment properly. Thereafter progress became very rapid, for, previously, designing aeroplanes had been rather like learning to swim before going into the water.

In 1910-11 aviation was chiefly concerned with " meetings " all over Europe, at first ostensibly competitions, but later frankly exhibitions, for competitors were paid appearance-money, whether they won anything or not. Crack fliers made quite a good deal of money, and the desire to outshine one another certainly spurred aeroplane makers on to improve their machines.

Perhaps the most historic event of 1910 was the appearance of Mr. A. V. Roe's tractor biplane, which afterwards became known as the " Avro." This machine, which was the first biplane to have the engine in front, set a new fashion in design, and the fastest aeroplanes of to-day are its direct descendants.

In 1911 Lord Northcliffe offered a prize of £10,000 for an aeroplane race round Britain. Two Frenchmen, Lieut. de Conneau, of the French Navy, and Jules Védrines, formerly an aeroplane mechanic, finished close together in the order named, and the late S. F. Cody came in some days later on the only British-built machine to finish. Only one other competitor completed the course.

The history of British aviation from 1909 to 1914 is a splendid story of struggling against racial apathy. The whole Empire owes a deep debt of gratitude to those men who devoted their lives and their fortunes to developing British aeroplanes, so that when war had shown the paramount importance of aeroplanes, they were able to produce the best aeroplanes in the world, the fastest, the quickest climbing, the best weight-lifters, and the most easily handled. And little less credit is due to those officers who, as soon as they attained a position wherein they were able to have a free hand, took every possible step to procure the best machines which British ingenuity could produce.

Meantime, the French Government had encouraged French aeroplane designers with respectable orders for military and naval aeroplanes, and French financiers found the money with which to help French firms over bad times. The organisation of the French Service d'Aviation had not been perfected when the war began, but the mental agility and energy of the French put their Flying Service into excellent order in a very short time, and to-day it is a close thing between the French and British as to who has the best aeroplanes and pilots.

Germany began early, in her usual methodical way, to encourage the production of war aeroplanes. Big competitions, in the form of long-distance cross-country races, were subsidised by the Government, and German flying officers were not only permitted but encouraged to compete therein against the crack civilian pilots, with notable advantage to both. As a result, all the aeroplane records, except those for speed, were held in Germany before the war, and German aeroplanes have hardly suffered at all in the war from failure of their engines, a fault which has lost France and England many fine pilots.

Germany began the war with more aeroplanes than all the Allies put together, but though her aeroplanes have improved in quality they have not improved as rapidly as those of France and England. Consequently the Allies are now slightly in the ascendant as regards their aeroplanes. The real ascendancy of the Allies is in their pilots, for the German has never been a sportsman or even a decent horseman, whereas the French and British are both, and flying is a game which demands, above all, a sporting temperament.

By way of a finish it may be well to set down a few figures showing how aeroplanes have improved in performance. The

Year	Average Speed	High Speed	Average Height	Great Height	Average Distance (without stop)	Long Distance (without stop)	Average Duration (without stop)	Long Duration (without stop)
	miles per hour	miles per hour	feet	feet	miles	miles		hours
1909	40	50	100	1,000	10	100	20 min.	2
1914	60	80	4,000	10,000	50	300	1 hour	4
1916	80	120	10,000	18,000	200	400	3 hours	8

figures are approximately those of 1909, 1914, and 1916, and represent respectively what would have been considered a fair average performance or a very good performance in those years.

It is worth noting, however, that two specially built French racing machines, incapable of climbing, had each done 120 miles in one hour in 1913, and that several German aviators on slow weight-lifting machines had in 1914 flown for more than eighteen hours without descending, one of them remaining aloft for just over twenty-four hours. Also in 1914, a German aviator with a passenger flew from Berlin to Eggri Palanka, on the Turkish Frontier, 1,000 miles, without stopping. And another German had reached a height of 25,250 feet. These, however, were record performances on specially contrived machines.

Sketchy as this " revue " may be, I hope it may give some idea of how aeroplanes have progressed, and if it induces a few people to study the possibilities of aircraft more deeply the work will not have been in vain.

C. G. GREY,
(Editor of the " The Aeroplane.")

LANGLEY (American). Built in 1902-03, and flown in 1915.

The LANGLEY flying machine (or "aerodrome," as it was called by Professor Langley himself). This machine was built in 1902-03, and failed to fly owing to defective handling. In 1915 the machine was rescued from the Smithsonian Institute by Mr. Glenn H. Curtiss, and after being fitted with floats and properly "tuned up," was flown by Mr. Curtiss over Lake Keuka, as shown. It was driven by the original engine, designed by Mr. Manley, and by the original propeller.

The first WRIGHT machine to fly by engine-power (December 17th, 1903).

THE FIRST HUMAN FLIGHT.   Mr. Orville Wright flying the WRIGHT biplane on December 17th, 1903.   The pilot lay flat on his face on the lower plane to reduce head resistance.   The engine was a 12 h.p. Wright.

WRIGHT (American).   The first machine to achieve human flight.   This machine left the ground and flew under control on December 17th, 1903.

ELLEHAMMER (Danish).   Built in 1905 and flew in 1906.

On 12th September, 1906, this machine made the first free flight in Europe. On 28th June, 1908, it won the prize at Kiel for the first flight in Germany (distance, 47 metres). It was a tractor biplane with a revolving Ellehammer motor. It also had a pendulum seat as a stabilising device.

PISCHOFF-KOECHLIN (French).   Built during 1905-06.

Dates from the days when a box-kite was the elementary idea in design, and the accepted position of the aviator lying prone.

AVRO (British).   (1906). This 24 h.p. biplane, designed by A. V. Roe, was the first British machine to leave the ground.

SANTOS-DUMONT (Brazilian-French.)   Mr. Santos-Dumont making his famous flight at Bagatelle, near Paris, on Oct. 23rd, 1906. The first real flight in France.

Built in France, by Señor Santos-Dumont, a Brazilian, already famous as a balloonist and pilot of airships. Made first hops on August 22nd, 1906, and on October 23rd made a definite flight of 200 feet, thus winning the Archdeacon Cup.

He covered 220 metres in 21 seconds, on November 12th, and won the prize of 1,500 francs offered by the Aero Club of France for the first person to fly 100 metres.

The engine was an 8-cylinder Antionette of 50 h.p., weighing 70 lbs.

The lifting surface of the machine was 650 sq. feet, and the weight, including the pilot, 645 lbs.

AVRO (British). Built in 1907, and made short flights in 1908. Tractor triplane of only 9 h.p. This flew in Lea Marshes—the lowest horse power yet flown in Europe to the present day.

VOISIN (French). The first European aeroplanes to fly with any real success.

BLERIOT (French). Blériot IV was the first Blériot machine actually to fly. It was built in 1907 and made short flights in 1908.

VOISIN (French). Built in 1907 and flown successfully by M. Henry Farman in 1908. The machine shown won the Deutsch-Archdeacon Grand Prix, on January 13th, 1908, with a flight of 1 min. 28 secs. This was the first aeroplane built by the *Voisin Frères* and was the first machine to make a turn in the air. The small third plane was added later as an experiment by M. Farman.

CODY (British-American). Built in the Balloon Factory at Farnborough in 1908, and flew in 1909. The fore-runner of the machine which won the British military trials of 1912.

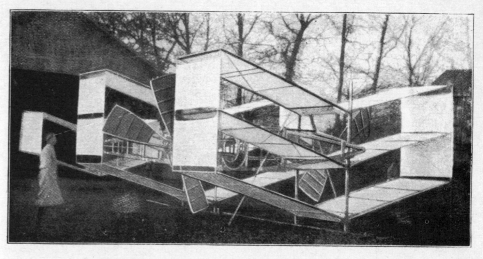

DUFAUX (Swiss). Built in 1908. The first Swiss attempt at an aeroplane.

CYGNET II (American-Canadian). A tetrahedral box-kite, designed by Dr. Graham-Bell of the Aeronautical Society of America, in conjunction with Mr. Glenn Curtiss, Mr. Herring, and Mr. Burgess. Made some few short straight flights.

ETRICH-WELS (Austrian). Built and flown by Herr Igo Etrich in 1908. The original of the *Etrich* "Taube" monoplanes which have done so much to make history. The first Austrian (and Germanic) machine to fly.

H. FARMAN (French). Mr. Henry Farman's first idea for a monoplane. About the first attempt at a tandem monoplane.

JUNE BUG (American-Canadian). Built by the Aeronautical Society of America and flown in 1908-09, by Mr. Glenn Curtiss (U.S.A.) and J. A. D. McCurdy (Canadian). Covered some 2,000 miles before being finally broken up.

GRADE (German). The first German aeroplane to fly.

MILLER (Italian). The first aeroplane designed and constructed by Italians.

PEMBERTON-BILLING (British). Built in 1908, and hopped variously in 1908-09. Lifted before wrecking itself. A very early example of a "pusher" monoplane.

R. E. P. (French). First example of a streamlined and enclosed body, and the first all-steel construction.

PISCHOFF-KOECHLIN (French). A very early example of a tractor biplane, and of upper plane extensions. The machine had also twin rudders.

VUIA (French). The first attempt to produce folding wings. It never flew.

WRIGHT BROS. (American). The first machine to fly real distances. Startled Europe by wonderful flights, piloted by Wilbur Wright, between August 1908, and April 1909, in France and Germany.

WITZIG-LIORÉ-DUTILLEUL (French). The first attempt at a "staggered" triplane.

ANTOINETTE IV (French). The machine on which the late M. Latham endeavoured to fly the Channel. In its day the best aeroplane in the world.

BLERIOT XI (French). The famous "Cross-Channel" type, and the forerunner of all the successful Bleriots). (Length, 23 feet. Span, 25¾ feet. Area, 167 sq. feet. Speed, about 45 m.p.h. Motor, 22-28 h.p. Anzani.

The Bleriot monoplane.

Photo by Jack Hunt

BLERIOT (French). The original BLERIOT monoplane on which M. Louis Bleriot flew from Calais to Dover on July 25th, 1909, with a 28 h.p. Anzani engine. The voyage took 37 minutes.

CHAUVIÉRE (French). An early example of a twin "pusher" monoplane with engine in front.

DE HAVILLAND (British). A very early twin "pusher" monoplane. Designed, built and flown by Mr. (now Captain) Geoffrey de Havilland, who has since designed many of the best British aeroplanes.

FARMAN (French). A typical HENRY FARMAN biplane (50 h.p. Gnome) of the Reims Meeting, August, 1909, with heavily loaded tail and big front elevator.

FRENCH MILITARY (French). A weird attempt on the part of French officialdom to produce a special military aeroplane. The planes were placed high above the body, so as to give the pilot a clear view below for reconnaissance, but it never lifted high enough for the view to be seen. It is an interesting example of official designs lagging behind private enterprise.

GABARDINI (Italian). A very early attempt to produce a flying boat, and ante-dating the *Fabre*.

PARSEVAL (German). The first German attempt at a flying-boat. Designed by Major von Parseval, of airship fame.

HOWARD WRIGHT (British). An all-steel biplane, the first "pusher" machine in which special attention was given to an enclosed "nacelle."

SANTOS-DUMONT (Brazilian-French). "La Demoiselle," the first attempt to build a small, light, cheap aeroplane for "the man of moderate means," and obviously of still more moderate weight. Its surface was only 9 sq. metres and its h.p. about 20. With exceptionally light pilots, such as M. Santos himself, and M. Audemars, it flew, and raised a speed of over 60 m.p.h.

DUNNE-HUNTINGTON (British). One of the earliest, if not the first, inherently stable aeroplanes. Designed by Mr. J. W. Dunne, the Wiltshire Regiment, in 1905-06, previous to secret experiments on behalf of the War Office, on the Duke of Atholl's Scottish estate, when it was tried as a glider by Colonel (now General) Capper and Mr. Dunne. The machine illustrated was built by Short Bros., Professor Huntington, and Mr. Dunne, at Leysdown, in 1909-10, and was still flying in 1913.

AVRO (British). The old *Avro* triplane, with 35 h.p. Green engine, carrying a passenger, piloted by Mr. A. V. Roe.

BREGUET IV (French). The first success of the famous Bréguet series. Nick-named the "coffee pot." In Aug., 1910, made a world's record by carrying six people, and proved itself superior in stability to anything of its period.

FARMAN (French). The first *Maurice Farman* biplane. Produced by M. Maurice Farman on his own account before the amalgamation of the interests of Mm. Henry and Maurice Farman.

FERGUSON (Irish). A small monoplane with J.A.P. engine, built by Mr. Harry Ferguson, of Belfast, in 1910. First left the ground and was smashed on landing late in December of that year. Was rebuilt and flown in 1911 and 1912. The only Irish machine which has flown.

LOOSE (American). An attempt to obtain lift by forcing air from twin tractors under arched wings. A favourite notion with inventors before, and ever since, up to the present day.

HERRING-BURGESS (American). An attempt to secure lateral stability by means of fins on top, in the manner tried three years later by the Royal Aircraft Factory, and rendered unnecessary by given a dihedral angle to the main planes.

MOISSANT (French-American). Built in Paris by the late Mr. Moissant. Wings of corrugated aluminium in the hopes of stopping "side-slip."

SHORT (British). The first machine of Short Brothers' own design, built for Mr. (now Major) J. T. C. Moore-Brabazon, and flown by him with a Green engine when winning the "Daily Mail" £1,000 prize for the first mile flown over a closed circuit on an all-British aeroplane.

VALKYRIE (British). The first, and almost the only, successful "tail first" monoplane. Built by Mr. (now Captain) Horatio Barber on Salisbury Plain, and subsequently flown by him in various parts of England.

SHORT (British). An early *Short* biplane, with 60 h.p. E.N.U. engine, big front elevator, and monoplane tail. This machine appeared at various meetings during 1910.

WRIGHT (American). The *Wright* biplane of 1910, to which a tail-elevator and rudder had been added. The machine shown is that on which the late the Hon. C. S. Rolls was killed at Bournemouth.

AVRO (British). The "Circuit of Britain" *Avro*, with E.N.V. engine. Smashed on day of race. An early example of a fixed-engine tractor biplane.

ANTOINETTE (French). The famous *Antoinette* monoplane, flown by the late M. Latham, at Brooklands, in 1912, though actually built in 1911. Probably the most beautiful aeroplane ever designed.

AVRO (British-Portuguese). Constructed to the ideas of a Portuguese officer, the fin on the top being intended to give lateral stability. A similar idea will be found among the Spanish military machines.

AVRO (British). An *Avro* with a 35 h.p. Green engine, fitted with floats, for Commander Schwann, R.N. Flew off the water with him in 1911, but was smashed. Later was flown by Mr. Sippe at Barrow-in-Furness. The first machine to get off British sea water.

Commander Schwann's *Avro* at Barrow-in-Furness.

BLERIOT (French). The "fish-tailed" *Blériot* of 1911-12. The pilot and passenger sat side by side.

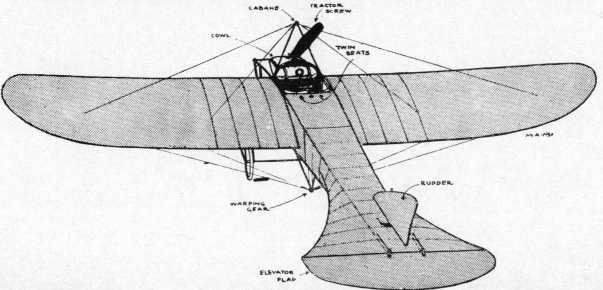

General arrangement of the 1911-12 " fish-tail " *Blériot*, which possessed several points embodied in the latest
Albatros machines, especially the " one piece " elevator, and the rudders post well forward in the fuselage.

BLERIOT (French).   Above, a single-seater high-speed version of the "fish-tail" type.   Below, a curious experimental "canard" or "tail-first" monoplane.

BLACKBURN (British). A *Blackburn* monoplane of the " Circuit of Britain " period, showing also method of mounting the Gnôme engine.

DANTON (French). The first tractor biplane with a backward " stagger " to the planes.

BOREL (French). The *Morane-Borel* monoplane (50 h.p. Gnôme engine) on which M. Jules Védrines won the " Circuit of Britain " race.

DE MARCAY-MOONEN (French). The first practicable aeroplane with folding wings. A hydro-biplane of the same type flew at Monaco in 1913.

DUNNE (British). The *Dunne* inherently stable monoplane, the only machine of its type ever built. It had all the stability of the biplane by the same designer.

DUIGAN (Australian).   The first Australian-built aeroplane to fly.   Built by Mr. J. R. Duigan, at Mia-Mia, and flown by him
in 1911.

FARMAN *(French).* The first *Henry Farman* biplane without a front elevator, and with pilot and passenger seated out in front of the lower plane.

FARMAN *(French).* A " racing " *Henry Farman* biplane of 1911, with 50 h.p. Gnôme engine, much used at Brooklands. This machine, originally the property of Mr. Snowden Smith, later of Mr. Maurice Ducrocq, and later of Mr. Pemberton-Billing, was taken over by the Navy at the beginning of the war, and was finally smashed by a pupil in 1915, at Chingford.

GRADE (German). A German version of the Santos-Dumont *Demoiselle*, with the pilot below the planes, and practically on the wheel axle.

GNOSSPELIUS (British). Built by Mr. Oscar Gnosspelius at Bowness-on-Windermere. Practically a *Bleriot*, with a big central float. Lifted at first attempt, but owing to inexperience of pilot and scarcity of power, fell in again, instead of alighting, and was damaged. Later flew well.

JEZZI (British). An early twin-tractor biplane, and about the first example of scientifically streamlined interplane struts.

LOHNER-DAIMLER (Austrian). The *Lohner* " Pfeil-Flieger," the first Austrian tractor biplane.

MACFIE (British).   The fore-runner of all "scout" biplanes.   Built in August, 1911, by Mr. R. F. Macfie to prove the possibilities of a small fast single-seater.   It was intended that the pilot's head should project above the upper plane.   The gap and chord were extremely small.   Unfortunately the machine was never finished.

NIEUPORT (French).   A typical *Nieuport* of the 1912-13 model.   The *Nieuport* has always been one of the fastest and most strongly built machines in the world.

NIEUPORT (French).   The typical *Nieuport* monoplane (50 h.p. Gnôme engine), which was at that time the fastest aeroplane in the world.

HANDLEY-PAGE (British). Built in 1911. Flew successfully through London from Barking to Brooklands, with a 50 h.p. Gnôme engine, piloted by the late Edward Petre. One of the first serious attempts in England to obtain inherent stability. Its likeness to the typical German "Taube" of the 1913-14 is worthy of note.

PAULHAN-FABRE (French). The curious biplane designed by M. Fabre, and built by M. Paulhan out of the proceeds of the London-Manchester flight. The spars were uncovered girders of flat wood, and the wing surface was held on flexible ribs like the trailing edge of a *Caudron*. The machine was largely held together by wire lashings instead of metal strips, and was a regular nautical job. It was, however, at best only an interesting freak.

PAULHAN-TATIN (French). The curious "torpedo" monoplane designed by M. Tatin and built by M Paulhan for the French military trials of 1911. The pilot sat in the front of the wings with the engine in his back, and the propeller was behind the tail, driven by a long shaft. The speed was about 90 m.p.h. and the machine was the fastest thing in the air, but it was very difficult to handle, and was never developed further.

R.E.P. (French). The *R.E.P.* monoplane flown by M. Gibert, in the "European Circuit." This machine flew from Paris to Amsterdam, Brussels, Calais, London, and back to Paris, without changing its engine.

VOISIN (French). The *Voisin* amphibian "canard," which made several successful flights starting from and alighting on the Seine, and the aerodrome of Issy-les-Moulineaux. It was the only "tail-first" hydro-aeroplane.

VALKYRIE (British). The *Valkyrie* "racer" with a 50 h.p. Gnôme, built and flown by Mr. H. C. Barber, was the most successful "tail-first" machine ever produced, and the only one which ever made long cross-country flights. Its best performance was a trip to Brighton and back with a passenger.

WATERHEN (British). A "pusher" hydro-biplane, built by the Lakes Flying Co., at Bowness-on-Windermere. First flew on November 25th, 1911. Was the first British aeroplane to fly off water and alight safely thereon. It was still flying in 1916, although little of the original material could have remained.

AVRO (British). The totally enclosed *Avro* biplane, starting for the first flight made in the British Military Trials of 1912, piloted by the late Lieut. Parke, R.N.

The totally enclosed *Avro* biplane (60-80 h.p.) Green engine, of the 1912 Military Trials.

AVRO (British). One of the first of the famous 50 h.p. Gnôme *Avros*, used in the early days of the R.F.C.

AVIATIK (German). An early *Aviatik* monoplane on the lines of the early French *Hanriot*. One of the first successful German aeroplanes.

B.E. (British). The first *B.E.* (British Experimental) biplane. Built and flown by Mr. Geoffrey de Havilland, then of the Royal Aircraft Factory. Performed well (*hors concours*) at the Military Aeroplane Trials.

BOREL (French).   The *Borel* "pusher" monoplane, one of the few machines ever built of this type, and the first to fly satisfactorily.

BREGUET (French).   A *Bréguet* with a 100 h.p. Gnôme engine, in the air.

BREGUET (French). A *Bréguet* biplane with 90 h.p. Salmson engine.

CODY (British). The late Mr. S. F. Cody making one of his favourite manœuvres on the machine, with an 80 h.p. Green engine, on which he won the Michelin Cup.

Back view of the *Cody* monoplane.

CODY (British). The only example of a *Cody* monoplane. Built by Mr. Cody for the Military Trials, with a 120 h.p. Austro-Daimler engine. It was utterly unlike anything else, having a dart-shaped body, and rudders quite independent of it. The machine was smashed just before the Trials, and the biplane which won the Trials was substituted for it at the last moment.

CODY (British). The *Cody* biplane, with 120 h.p. Austro-Daimler engine, which won the British Military Aeroplane Competition and the £5,000 first prize.

FARMAN (French). A typical *Maurice Farman* "longhorn" biplane, with 70 h.p. Renault engine. One of the most satisfactory types of aeroplane ever produced, and still largely used for elementary training by the R.F.C.

FOKKER (German-Dutch). The first machine built by Mijnheer Fokker, a young Dutchman who later became famous as the designer and builder of the *Fokker* "chasers." This machine was absolutely inherently stable and had no lateral control fitted to it. It was inspected in Germany in 1912 by British officers, but was so badly made that they very properly refused to recommend its purchase.

HANRIOT (French). The small Gordon-Bennett *Hanriot* monoplane. An early example of extreme reduction of head-resistance.

MARTINSYDE (British). The big _Martinsyde_ monoplane of 1912, with 60 h.p. Antoinette engine. The handsomest machine of its day.

MERSEY (British). The *Mersey* monoplane (60 h.p. Isaacson), the first British monoplane with engine in front and propeller behind.

PAGE (British). The *Handley Page* monoplane of 1912, built for the Military Trials, with a 70 h.p. Gnôme, but not finished in time. It was one of the early examples of an inherently stable machine, with swept-back wings.

SHORT (British). The famous S 38 type *Short* biplane, 50 h.p. Gnôme, largely used for instructional purposes by the R. N. A. S. in 1912-13-14-15 & 16. In its day one of the most comfortable and safest flying machines ever produced, but too slow for modern ideas.

SHORT (British). The first *Short* tractor-biplane of ordinary type, the fore-runner of the big *Short* seaplanes.

SHORT (British). The typical *Short* " pusher " biplane, with Gnôme engine, of the kind largely used for training in the early days at Eastchurch.

SHORT (British). The *Short* biplane, on the launching platform of H.M.S. "Hibernia," from which the first flight by an aeroplane from a moving vessel was made by Lieut. C. R. Sampson, R.N., on May 4th, 1912.

SHORT (British). The first flight in the world from the deck of a moving ship. Lieut. Sampson, R.N., leaving the forecastle of H.M.S. "Hibernia," on May 4th, 1912.

SOPWITH (British). A *Sopwith* "bat-boat" with 90 h.p.
Austro-Daimler. The first British flying boat.

SOPWITH (British). The first British-built *Sopwith* biplane. A copy of an American *Wright*, but with a 40 h.p.
A.B.C. engine and a closed nacelle. Piloted by Mr. H. C. Hawker, it won the Michelin Cup Prize of 1912.

AGO (German). The *Ago* "pusher" biplane, with 6 cylinder 100 h.p. Argus engine.

BOSSI (Italian). The first Italian hydro-aeroplane to fly with marked success.

BRÉGUET (French).   A big hydro-biplane, with a 200 h.p. Salmson engine, which performed magnificently at Monaco in March, 1913.   Won the " Grand Prix " in a gale, and was wrecked after alighting.   Had four floats and a flexible under-carriage.   Was the first machine to deserve the name of seaplane.   If it had had efficient wings it would probably have been the equal of any seaplane existing to-day.

54

DEPERDUSSIN (Franco-British). The famous *Deperdussin* monoplane designed by Mr. Koolhoven and flown by Lieut. J. C. Porte, R.N., at Hendon. With a 100 h.p. Anzani engine it was one of the fastest machines of its period. It was laid up during most of 1914, but was taken over by the Navy on the outbreak of war, and was flown regularly, at any rate, as late as 1916 by naval officers on long cross-country journeys.

DEUTSCHE FLUGZEUG WERKE (German). Typical *D.F.W.* aeroplanes.   At top, the *D.F.W.* biplane, 120 h.p. Austro-Daimler motor, as used by the German army. Below, the *D.F.W.* monoplane, winner of the 1913 Prinz Heinrich Preis, and used in the early part of the war. At bottom, a variant in wing design of the same machine.

DUNNE (British).   View from behind, in front, and below of the *Dunne* biplane, evolved by Mr. J. W, Dunne from experiments with gliders in 1905-06.   The machine is absolutely inherently stable.   Though now non-existent in England, it is still made successfully by the Burgess Co. in America.

FARMAN (French). The "F-24" *Henry Farman* biplane, a curious freak of little practical value, but of some interest as the embryo of a type which may be developed in big scale aeroplanes.

GRADE (German). A curious little monoplane built purely for aerobatics, and designed to alight upside down, as a circus trick.

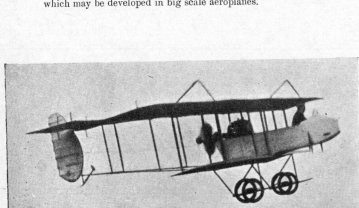

FARMAN (French). A typical *Henry Farman* biplane of 1913, with 80 h.p. Gnôme engine.

FRIEDRICHSHAFEN (German). An amphibious "pusher" biplane, built by the Friederichshafen Flugzeugbau, a branch of the Zeppelin Co.

JEANNIN (German). The *Jeannin Stahltaube* (Steel Dove). A monoplane built entirely of steel as regards the frame-work, the usual fabric covering was, of course, used over it.

GRAHAME-WHITE (British). A typical *Grahame-White* "pusher" biplane (50 h.p. Gnôme engine) of the design familiar to all visitors to Hendon. On machines of this type and modifications thereof an immense number of R.N.A.S. and R.F.C. pilots have been trained.

MARTINSYDE (British). The *Martinsyde* monoplane with Austro-Daimler engine, of 1913. One of the most graceful aeroplanes of its day. Although not designed as a racing machine, its speed was close on 90 miles an hour, and piloted by Mr. Harold Barnwell, it finished second within a second or two of the late Mr. Gustav Hamel, on a small racing *Morane*, in the " Circuit of London " race, early in 1914.

MORANE (French). The *Morane* hydro-monoplane on which Mr. Claude Grahame-White flew from Paris to Putney.

NORTHERN AIRCRAFT CO. (British). The N.A.C. " pusher " monoplane, here seen fitted with a single central float, and an 80 h.p. Gnôme engine, was built in 1913 by the Northern Aircraft Co., Ltd., of Windermere (since defunct), to designs by Mr. W. H. Sayers and Mr. G. Gnosspelius. It is the only example of a monoplane " pusher " waterplane.

RADLEY-ENGLAND (British). An interesting seaplane, designed by Mr. Gordon England, for the "Daily Mail" Seaplane Circuit.   It had three 50 h.p. Gnome engines fitted to one shaft, driving by chains an overhead propeller-shaft.   The pilot sat in one float and the passenger in the other.   It was smashed in a collision with a buoy, and could not be rebuilt in time for the competition.   Below it is seen after the collision.

ROYAL AIRCRAFT FACTORY (British). One of the early F.E. biplanes, with Renault engine, built by the Royal Aircraft Factory in 1913. It suffered from too big a nose and too little vertical area aft, having a comparatively small rudder and no fixed vertical fin, which made it very evil to fly in any wind. Owing to arguments concerning the death of a passenger on this machine much attention was drawn to the question of "fin area," and the liability of badly designed machines to "spin" uncontrollably.

SANCHEZ-BESA (Franco-Brazilian). A Biplane, with 80 h.p. Gnôme engine geared down.

SOPWITH (British). A *Sopwith* "tabloid" scout of 1913 landing. This was the type of machine which first demonstrated that a biplane not only has a wider range of speed than a monoplane, but can be faster. This machine showed a range of speed from 45 to 95 miles an hour, with an 80 h.p. Gnôme engine.

SHORT (British). The four-seater *Short* seaplane (160 h.p. 14-cylinder Gnôme engine) on which Messrs. McClean, Short, Ogilvie and Spottiswoode variously journeyed from Cairo to Khartoum up the Nile during the summer of 1913.

SHORT (British). An experimental *Short* biplane with two 80 h.p. Gnôme engines. One in front driving two tractor-screws by chains, and one behind driving a propeller. A machine much used experimentally by naval pilots.

SOPWITH (British). The *Sopwith* amphibian "bat-boat," which, piloted by Mr. H. G. Hawker and with a 100 h.p Green engine, won the Mortimer Singer Prize for a series of flights starting from land and alighting on water, and *vice versa*. It is here shown getting off the water and alighting on land. The wheels were movable, so that they could be raised for operation on water and lowered while in the air for land work.

SOPWITH (British). The *Sopwith* "Tabloid." The fore-runner of all the small high-speed "scout," "fighter" and "pup" biplanes of to-day. Its appearance early in 1913 revolutionised all ideas of speed and climbing rate

THOMAS (American). A *Thomas* biplane of 1913, about the first American aeroplane to approximate to the modern European type of "pusher" biplane.

VOISIN (French). An early *Voisin* hydro-biplane with 80 h.p. Gnôme engine.

J. S. WHITE & Co. (British). The *Wight* seaplane, 160 h.p. 14-cylinder Gnôme, which put up the best performance for any seaplane of its power at that period.

AVRO (British). One of the three famous 80 h.p. Gnome *Avros* (of the 1913-14 type) about to start from Belfort on the historic raid, in November, 1914, when the Zeppelin Factory at Friederichshafen was bombed and damaged.

B.E. 2. An interesting experimental *B.E.*, built by the Royal Aircraft Factory before the war, with an oleo-pneumatic landing gear. This was one of the first inherently stable *B.E.'s*.

CAPRONI (Italian). A *Caproni* monoplane with 80 h.p. Gnome, one of the most successful of pre-war Italian machines.

DE BOLOTOFF (Russo-French). This triplane was begun by Prince Serge de Bolotoff, at Mourmelon, in 1908, and remained in process of construction in France and at Brooklands, till the outbreak of war. The photographs were taken late in 1914, before and after an attempt to fly, in which it failed. It is worth placing on record as one of those "mystery" machines in which many people of note were interested, without seeing their hopes realised.

DEUTSCHE FLUGZEUG WERKE (German). The *D.F.W.* high-speed Scout, 100 h.p. Mercédés, used on active service, and breaker of all cross-country records just before the outbreak of war. The side panels between the wings have since been discarded. The cabane arrangement is practically the same as the "1½ Strutter" *Sopwith*. It was originally designed by Mr. Cecil Kny, and is the first example of a carefully streamlined German aeroplane.

FARMAN (French).   One of the earliest "Shorthorn" *Maurice Farmans*   A type still largely used on active service and for training of pilots.

HALL (British).   An interesting example of the combination of the *Caudron* wing structure with an ordinary fuselage. A very effective school machine.

PAGE (British).   The *Handley Page* biplane of 1914, almost the only example of a British biplane with swept-back wings to procure inherent stability.

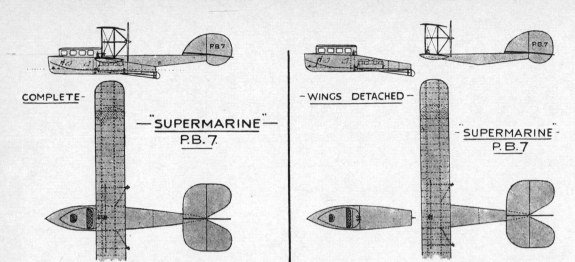

COMPLETE-

-WINGS DETACHED-

"SUPERMARINE"
P.B.7

-SUPERMARINE-
P.B.7

(Designs for projected "Supermarine.")

PEMBERTON-BILLING (British). The Supermarine, illustrated, is a projected design for a flying boat of large or small size, intended to shed its wings and tail on alighting on the water, and become a seaworthy motor boat, the reason being that a seaplane with a disabled engine presents so much surface to the waves, and so is wrecked because of its flying surfaces, despite the boat portion. The system also has much to recommend it for large passenger vehicles, the boat coming alongside a pier to pick up passengers, and afterwards locking up with its wings, which are moored in the open. Boats for this type of machine were actually ready for the fitting of the wings when war broke out and work on them was stopped.

RUMPLER (German). The *Rumpler* military type biplane, which just before the war broke various distance and duration records, including an 18 hours non-stop flight by Herr Basser, and a flight from Berlin to Constantinople, stopping only at Vienna, Sofia, and Bucharest. Herr Basser is seen in the pilot's seat above. The fuselage and engine were the same as those with which Herr Linnekögel beat the world's height record, but the machine was then a monoplane, and it was afterwards turned into a biplane, so that it could carry the big load of fuel for an attempt to fly for 24 hours. The same 100 h.p. Mercédés engine was used in all its flights.

SOPWITH (British). A big *Sopwith* "bat-boat," 200 h.p. Salmson engine, of the type supplied just before the war to Germany, and also to the Greek Navy. One of the finest seaplanes ever produced, but did not find favour in England.

SANCHEZ-BESA (French-Brazilian).   The *Sanchez-Besa*
biplane of 1913, precursor of the all-steel *Voisins* of the war period.

VICKERS (British).   Vickers' "gun-carrier" biplane, 1914-15 type.   The first real fighting aeroplane.

VICKERS   (British). One of the first of the Vickers' gun-carriers, which with Monosoupape Gnôme engines, did such good work in the early days of 1915.

WRIGHT (American). An interesting photograph of Mr. Alec. Ogilvie Wright, on a *Wright* glider, performing the feat of soaring. This machine, which had no engine, was launched from the top of a sand-bank and remained in the air for 9 minutes by soaring in the up-current blowing from the sea.

B. E. (British). A typical *B.E.* biplane, with 70 h.p. Renault engine, of late 1914 or early 1915 type. Photographed from another machine.

CURTISS (American).   The standard type *J. N.*
Curtiss biplane, with 90 h.p. Curtiss engine, on which so many
British aviators learned to fly in the early days of the war.

FOKKER (German-Dutch).   A typical *Fokker* monoplane, with Oberursel engine.   The type of machine, which
did so much valuable defensive work as a " chaser " or " destroyer " over the German lines during the latter part of 1915 and
the first half of 1916.

SHORT (British). One of the famous *Short* seaplanes, with 100 h.p Gnôme engines. which have operated in all war areas. This one was photographed at Durban prior to going up to German East Africa to look for the "Königsberg."

SHORT (British). One of the early 225 h.p. Sunbeam *Short* seaplanes. A type which has done much work in all theatres of war.

SOPWITH (British).   A *Sopwith* seaplane, with 10) h.p. Gnôme engine, being tested before flying, on the coast of
German East Africa.

FOKKER (German).   The first *Fokker* biplane.   It is here seen on service in the Carpathians, during the
Austrian advance.

The famous aerodrome of Johannisthal, near Berlin, as it was about 1912. A *Parseval* passenger airship is seen above and an *Aviatik-Farman* below. The huge grand stand shows how seriously the Germans considered aviation even in those days.

AN AERONAUTICAL DICTIONARY AND SOME MEMORANDA.

[The following dictionary of some 300 technical and slang terms does not profess to be absolutely complete, but in it will be found practically all unusual words necessarily to be comprehended by those who wish to understand the ordinary written or spoken language of those concerned with Aircraft. Many of the words will be found illustrated in the accompanying drawings of "Pusher" and "Tractor" biplanes.—C. G. G.]

Index